MW00713546

A WAR AGAINST TERROR THROUGH MY LENS

A WAR AGAINST TERROR THROUGH MY LENS

ALBERT M. STARK

To order additional copies of this book, contact:
Xlibris Corporation ·
1-888-795-4274
www.Xlibris.com
Orders@Xlibris.com
29780

CONTENTS

To Jared and Rachel

AUTHOR'S NOTE

As the fifth anniversary of September 11, 2001 approached, I recalled the night I sang blessings and lit three Hanukkah candles ten years before. After my son, Jared, slid a gift-wrapped package toward me, I tore the wrapping paper and found a black sketchbook with empty, unlined pages. "What do I do with this?" I asked. His whimsical expression did not change. "I cannot draw a straight line," I added.

"Remember our conversation?"

Two weeks earlier, our hearts pumped as we glided over ten miles of narrow cross-country trails beneath an azure blue sky in Park City, Utah. Resting in front of a crackling fire, he inquired, "Dad, what regrets do you have?"

"That I have not been able to write about what I have experienced," I replied.

"Now you can begin."

I RIFLED THROUGH MY LAW DIARIES, GOT UP EARLY IN THE MORNING AND WROTE ABOUT MY LAW CASES IN THE SKETCHBOOK, NOW A JOURNAL BOOK. MY BOOK *Beyond the Bar – Challenges in a Lawyer's Life* was born. All the while, I wrote about my life and events as I saw them. Like most people, I got a sense of current events and the time in which I live from the mass media. Mass media feeds on hot stories. Today's headlines and news stories are forgotten quickly because memories are short.

In this memoir, I have written about events from 1991 to 2005 as I saw them. I hope it is like a photo album, which after you look at snapshots, a bigger picture of your life and time develops, giving you a better appreciation of the past and its meaning. Sharing with the reader my views as I described them in my journal book, I hope to shed light on the age of terror in which we live and encourage readers to examine the terror in their lives and how they fight it. Hopefully, some of my readers will heed some of the lessons my life has taught me and give birth to a movement that will lead to a fight against terror on a different battlefield from that on which it is being fought today.

LIFE THROUGH LENSES

The lens through which one sees the world is shaped by life experiences. In January 1993, my son, Jared, and daughter, Rachel, described their Sunday morning childhood visits to Cadwalader Park in Trenton. "We stood on one side of a fence and fed the deer standing on the other," Jared said. "What was it that the deer saw?" Rachel asked family and friends celebrating Grandpa Sidney's eighty-fifth birthday. Their answer – "a Grandpa with Wonder Bread standing behind two children." Jared handed Grandpa Sidney a gift-wrapped box as Rachel told Grandpa Sidney he symbolized kindness, empowerment, guidance, and humor.

Smiling, Grandpa Sidney unwrapped the gift and pulled a camera from its box and held it up for all to see. "Our gift is a camera," Jared and Rachel said, "because a camera is a symbol of seeing life from another lens."

When I fastened my seat belt on a plane bound for Portugal on September 10, 2001, I did not know that the next day I would be walking around Lisbon with a heavy heart and a racing mind because newsclips showed a hijacked jetliner crashing into a tower of the World Trade Center in New York and smoke billowing from the Pentagon in Washington and a field in western Pennsylvania into which another hijacked plane plummeted before it struck the United States Capitol. The targets – all symbols of the economic and military might of the United States.

September 11, 2001, was a sad day not only because the World Trade Center towers, ablaze, collapsed, not only because video cameras captured men and women in business suits plummeting from the upper floors, eighty to one hundred stories above the streets, and not only because three thousand innocents lost their lives, but also because the free world would soon suffer loss of freedoms, impediments to movement and travel because men, rather than laws, would determine the actions that would follow. The

11

lens through which the world would see our leaders would not reveal our leaders to be Grandpa Sidneys.

The portion of the Old Testament I read at my bar mitzvah, Leviticus, chapter19, tells us that vengeance begets vengeance and that grudges breed hate. What would those words mean in the aftermath of September 11, 2001? "Cowards killed," so said the attacked. "The guilty must pay. Bravery will be remembered," so said the attackers.

In Portugal, I was less than a mile from where the Moors, who were Muslim, and Christians fought from AD 1100 to AD 1600. Throughout history, wars have been brutal.

The United States under the leadership of George W. Bush retaliated, bombing cities and villages in Afghanistan and the sites of training camps run by Osama bin Laden. Instead of declaring the hijackers and their sponsors criminals, and bringing them to justice in American courts, President George W. Bush declared war on terror wherever it took us. Would this one pit Christians against Muslims – a war that, if history repeated itself, would change the western world for generations?

Would retaliation and vengeance make life a lottery?

Through my lens I saw dangerous times ahead.

LENS LESSONS

What did Osama bin Laden, a fundamentalist Muslim from an established, well-to-do Saudi family, see through his lens? On a videotape filmed in a cave in the Tora Bora Mountains of Afghanistan, he described Saudi Arabia's role in the Gulf War as a "sellout" to western capitalistic values.

When I was on vacation in Switzerland in 1979, Saudi sheiks sat in salons in Switzerland, their heads covered in kerchiefs, armed guards at their sides as they fingered diamond-studded gold watches and then forked over wads of cash, profits made from the oil crisis of the 1970's that could have fed many Arabs. Surely, bin Laden witnessed what I had.

After bin Laden was identified as the "coward" by George W. Bush, I was repulsed by the thought that the Saudi king, controlling the world's oil supply, had abused and neglected his poor subjects. The frustration of millions of unemployed, hungry, and restless fed bin Laden's movement. If only the Saudi King had been a Grandpa Sidney, who fed them, empowered them, guided and nurtured them. Now bin Laden was the villain in the September 11 story.

The hijackers bin Laden recruited were intelligent, skilled young men willing to give their lives to promote bin Laden's announced goal – to destroy Western civilization to gain control of the Middle East and place it under the rule of Muslim fundamentalism, ridding the area of wealthy princes in Saudi Arabia, the United Arab Emirates, Dubai, and Qatar, and ridding the Middle East of Israel, a symbol of western civilization.

On September 24, 2001, a Gallup poll showed that George W. Bush, a president who was floundering before September 11, now had an approval rating of 92 percent.

To bin Laden, Americans were blind to the root cause of the World Trade Center disaster – the crime of poverty. To bin Laden, George W. Bush was the heir to the Ronald Reagan and George H. W. Bush policies that prioritized oil, oil, and oil over people and tax cuts for the wealthy.

The Communists – Lenin, Trotsky, and Marx – set out to do what bin Laden espoused. Look what happened. Corruption created a ruling class, which was deposed in a revolution.

Would bin Laden and his followers feed and educate the flock on the other side of the fence? Would Muslim fundamentalists be any different from those who were in power?

Throughout the world, cameras snapped pictures of the protagonists and antagonists. Who was which one was to be determined through whose lens one looked.

RUDE AWAKENING

After I returned from Portugal in early October, I read the journals that I kept during the 1990s. I peered at snapshots of events.

A Secret Service crew installed a satellite dish on the roof to set up a command post with three telephones in a conference room in my law office. A black telephone was labeled AF1, a red one AF2, and a white one WH. Four men wearing black jackets with SECRET SERVICE on their backs held leashes attached to German shepherd dogs as they roamed my law office, sniffing corners and under desks. It was a Thursday in June 1992.

Vice President Dan Quayle was coming to Trenton the following Monday to promote urban education and diversity initiatives. As a favor to a Republican client, the Stark & Stark law firm agreed to host a meeting where the vice president could meet influential Republicans. The office was convenient because it was located at an exit of I-95, a short distance from Mercer County Airport, where Air Force 2 would land.

I had a flashback to 1988. I was visiting the Soviet Union on a "people-to-people" trip. I laughed at the the Muscovite, who likened himself to a dog on a leash,who told me, "I can bark, but I cannot get food to eat." At a rally of the Green Party in Riga, Latvia, I thought that the hungry voices of discontent calling from the desert would be heard.

Mikhail Gorbachev was a breath of fresh air. Gorby appeared to be a leader, who with glasnost and peristroika, would lead the Soviet Union to a position of great influence, heralding a banner of individual freedom. Even though people were standing in line to get food and storefronts were bare, people seemed hopeful. Through my lens, Gorby looked like a Grandpa Sidney. But from 1988 to 1992, Gorby traveled the world extolling freedom of speech, but did little to reduce the food lines.

Shortly after noon on Monday, snipers positioned themselves on the roof and behind an air-conditioning compressor. Sirens wailed as police cars led a caravan of black SUVs with opaque windows into the parking lot in front of the office. The vice president, surrounded by a cordon of men wearing dark sports jackets and earphones, made his way toward the office, followed by press personnel with notebooks in their hands. He cast a glance at a small group of union members holding signs – We want Work not War – and waved.

I greeted the vice president at the entrance and ushered him to a conference room in which twenty-five people who had donated at least $1,000 to the Bush-Quayle campaign, waited. He was coming from a visit to an elementary school in Trenton that was attended by students who were predominantly African-American and Hispanic.

One of my partners escorted the press corps to a table set up with sandwiches and beverages. Even though I was a Democrat, I had hope. I thought that Bush and Quayle had heard the cries of millions of impoverished Americans, who were crying for opportunity in education and diversity, that he and George H.W. Bush had seen what was happening to Gorby and heard the cries of the needy and had decided to become Grandpa Sidneys. After the guests shook hands with Vice President Quayle and exchanged a few words, the group took seats around a conference table and listened to the vice president extol the Bush administration's success in the Gulf War and their tax cuts for business. "Our approval rating is 92 percent," he said. "This is going to be a boring election campaign. Victory in November is assured."

A Secret Service agent rapped on the conference room door.

"Does anyone know where I can find a dictionary?" he inquired.

I took the Secret Service agent to my office where he thumbed through the pages until he reached the word *potato*.

That morning, the vice president had participated in a spellng bee at the Luis Munoz School. He asked a sixth grader to spell *potato*. Twelve-year-old William Figueroa wrote P-O-T-A-T-O on the blackboard. Quayle looked at a flash card given to him and insisted that *potato* was spelled with an E at the end – P-O-T-A-T-O-E.

Since the press corps had been excluded from the meeting with the fat cat donors, they got into a conversation about the correct spelling of *potato*. When Quayle finished the meeting, he went into the office lobby and met with the press. "Any questions?" he asked.

"How do you spell potato?" one inquired.

"P-O-T-A-T-O-E," the vice president replied. Laughter filled the lobby.

Evening newscasts and the next day's newspapers featured clips and headlines VEEP CAN'T SPELL. There were no newsclips about diversity or education. Quayle became the butt of political jokes. Quayle's visit to the Luis Munoz School was the last Bush-Quayle event that promoted educational opportunity and diversity. Looking back, the Day of the Potatoe was the beginning of the end of the presidency of George Herbert Walker Bush.

As 1992 ended, people asked each other, "Who could have predicted Mikhail Gorbachev would be out of power in the Soviet Union or that George H. W. Bush would be defeated?" Both Gorbachev and Bush and Qualye failed to address the crime of poverty. Boris Yeltsin, Bill Clinton and Al Gore did.

During the second week of January 1993, I picked up the *New York Times*. The front page had three pictures. The first showed Ronald Reagan smiling, wearing a medal awarded to him by George H. W. Bush, a man with but seven days left in his presidency. In the second picture, Bush hugged Caspar Weinberger, the former secretary of defense. The look on Weinberger's face was one of quiet and relief, powerlessness and shame. The third picture captured Bush sitting alone on a sofa behind which were Vice President Dan Quayle, former secretary of state, James Baker, and head of the Joint Chiefs of Staff Brent Scowcroft – three whites symbolic of the Bush presidency; Quayle, the Howdy Doody puppet; Baker, the promoter; and Scowcroft, the implementer of the Bush love-or-hate agenda. Educational opportunity and diversity were nowhere in the picture.

To the Reagan and Bush Republicans, the loss of the White House was not only a surprise but also the destruction of their dream to create an American empire throughout the world – a New World Order. It was a rude awakening.

The '60s had been a decade when those out of power protested the way government and society worked. On the eve of the inauguration of Bill Clinton, those who had protested were now positioned to govern. Would the '90s be the '60s upside down?

Bernice Munce, the only African American teacher at Junior High School # Three, taught me in seventh grade that government should be of laws, not men. As a seventh grader, that meant that I could trust the government.

I believed our country followed that principle until 1960 when I was a senior at Dartmouth College. That was when my president, Dwight D. Eisenhower, whose every word I believed, lied to me, denying that a U-2 spy plane invaded the airspace of the Soviet Union. In fact, U-2 pilot Gary Powers had been shot down over the Soviet Union. I was betrayed and saw the incident as a rude awakening.

Still, as a child of the '60s, I thought I could change the world, to make life better for everyone – to achieve justice for all.

In my late twenties, I was president of the Trenton Junior Chamber of Commerce. I saluted the flag and recited the Jaycee Creed, which said that "the brotherhood of men transcends the sovereignty of nations; that economic justice can best be won by free men through free enterprise; that government should be of laws rather than of men; that earth's great treasure lies in human personality; and that service to humanity is the best work of life."

Now in 1993, I was fifty-four-years-old. The media focused on negative news, widespread corruption in government and business, the enormous challenges of poverty, the failure of our educational system, rising gang violence and ethnic conflict. Many were losing hope. I was not.

The world needed a clean example that our government is one of laws, not of men. As the government changed from Bush to William Jefferson Clinton, the country deserved a clean break from the politics as usual.

Through my lens, I gazed at the landscape and wondered. Would the generation which preached drinking water to others and now drank wine be able to create change? Would the new generation have the courage to cut the deficit, correct excesses of the past, and infuse schools with educational programs for two, three, and four-year-olds that were children of broken, uneducated families?

Three hundred thousand people graced the Washington Mall, caring, glad that an outsider had come in to scale down and reorganize the government to meet the needs of society and not just make corporations well-off. Could the new people in power overcome a fear that the country would head toward oligarchy where the wealthy would have to protect themselves? History told us that oligarchy was the last stage of a democracy before there was a revolution.

I watched the Clinton era begin. It was a balmy sunny morning filled with skepticism and hope. I related my 1960-1990 allegory to a high school friend. "If you look at the number 6 it is a straw that gets filled from the top. If you turn over the 6, it becomes a 9, and whatever filled it will flow out." I hoped that the values that filled the '60s – and the Jaycee Creed – caring, elimination of prejudice, equality, and creativity – would flow out as we headed toward the year 2000.

Sitting twenty rows in front of a podium on a stage in front of the United States Capitol, I felt poet Maya Angelou capture the mood of the land when she recited "The Rock Cries Out to Us Today."

A Rock, A River, A Tree,
Hosts to species long since departed,
Marked the mastodon,
The dinosaur, which left dried tokens,
Of their sojourn here
On our planet floor,
Any broad alarm of their hastening doom,
Is lost in the gloom and dust and ages.

But today, the Rock cries out to us, clearly,
Forcefully,
Come, you may stand upon my
Back and face your distant destiny,
But seek no haven in my shadow.
I will give you no hiding place down here.

You, created only a little lower than
The angels, have crouched too long in
The bruising darkness
Have lain too long
Face down in ignorance.
Your mouths spilling words.

Armed for slaughter.
The Rock cries out to us today, you may
Stand upon me
But do not hide your face.

Across the wall of the world,
A River sings a beautiful song. It says,
Come, rest here by my side.

Each of you, a bordered country,
Delicate and strangely made proud,
"Yet" thrusting perpetually under siege.
Your armed struggles for profit,
Have left collars of waste upon shore, currents of debris upon my breast.

Yet today I call you to my riverside,
If you will study war no more. Come,
Clad in peace, and I will sing the songs
The Creator gave to me when I and the
Tree and the rock were one.
Before cynicism was a bloody sear across
Your
Brow and when you yet knew you still
Knew nothing.
The River sang and sings on. (italics mine)

There is a true yearning to respond to
The singing River and the wise Rock.
So say the Asian, the Hispanic, the Jew
The African, the Native American, the Sioux,
The Catholic, the Muslim, the French, the Greek,
The Irish, the Rabbi, the Priest, the Sheik,
The Gay, the Straight, the Preacher,
The privileged, the homeless, the Teacher.
They hear. They all hear
The speaking of the Tree.

They hear the first and last of every Tree
Speak to humankind today. Come to me, here
Beside the River.
Plant yourself beside the River.

Each of you, descendant of some passed
On traveler, has been paid for.
You, who gave me my first name, you
Pawnee, Apache, Seneca, you
Cherokee Nation, who rested with me, then

Forced on bloody feet,
Left me to the employment of
Other seekers – desperate for gain,
Starving for gold.
You, the Turk, the Arab, the Swede, the
German, the Eskimo, the Scot.
You the Ashanti, the Yoruba, the Kru,
Bought,
Sold, stolen, arriving on the nightmare,
Playing for a dream.
Here, root yourselves beside me.
I am that Tree planted by the River,
Which will not be moved.
I, the Rock, I, the River, I, the Tree
I am yours – your passages have been paid.
Lift up your faces, you have a piercing need
For this bright morning dawning for you.
History, despite its wrenching pain,
Cannot be unlived, but if faced
With courage, need not be lived again.

Lift up your eyes upon,
This day breaking for you.
Give birth again
To the dream.

Women, children, men,

Take it into the palms of your hands,
Mold it into the shape of your most
Private need. Sculpt it into
The image of your most public self.
Lift up your hearts
Each new hour holds new chances
For a new beginning.
Do not be wedded forever
To fear, yoked eternally
To brutishness.

The horizon leans forward,
Offering you space to place new steps of
Change.
Here, on the pulse of this fine day
You may have the courage
To look up and out and upon me, the
Rock, the River, the Tree, your country.
No less to Midas than the mendicant.
No less to you now than the mastodon then.

Here, on the pulse of this new day,

You may have the grace to look up and out
And into your sister's eyes, and into
Your brother's face, your country
And say simply
Very simply
With hope –
Good morning.

I remembered young men standing in the ballroom of a downtown Trenton hotel at a Trenton Junior Chamber of Commerce meeting. I heard the words "That earth's great treasure lies in human personality; and that service to humanity is the best work of life." Oh, how I hoped that the world would stand up and repeat the Jaycee Creed and repeat Maya Angelou's poem. They were perfect prescriptions for what an effective war against terror would be.

Inspired and tired, I was leaving an inaugural ball late on January 20, 1993. I ran into Joe Merlino, president of the New Jersey Senate, who was my mentor in the Mercer County Prosecutor's Office. In 1981, he had run for governor of New Jersey. As Merlino's finance chairman, I saw that millions of dollars were needed to win an office that paid less than $100,000. Worse yet, it required at least $4,000,000 to get elected senator from New Jersey and $400,000 to win a seat in Congress. My idealist vision of public service clouded like a malfunctioning television screen. How could an elected official, even Bill Clinton, avoid the demands of special interests? Money was power and political power was the ability to influence men's minds. Would money control the generation that preached drinking water and now savored good wine?

A few days later, my father, Grandpa Sidney, sat in my office and reflected about what he saw through his lens. Born in 1908 and a child of turn-of-the-century America, he saw the '40s and '50s producing pride-in-America powerful cars, suburbia, superpolitical giants – the USSR and the USA – and the Cold War. Slow dancing gave way to rock 'n' roll, the Beatles, hippies, yippies, free love, drugs, individualism, free expression, civil rights, and civil disobedience. It bred crack babies, AIDS, a failing public education system in our cities because the new middle class deserted city schools, and a feeling of separation between suburban whites and urban blacks, Hispanics, Haitians, and miscellaneous minorities followed. He said, "The generation in the 1990s has to worry not about free love but safe sex. Not about civil rights but about unsafe streets where people carry mace and gun control is a top priority. The gas-guzzlers of the '50s and '60s are now dinosaurs, and foreign cars are economical."

We watched Senator Arlen Specter, who had brutally attacked Anita Hill after she accused George H.W. Bush's appointee, Clarence Thomas, of sexual harrassment. Now he attacked Zoe Baird, the first female to be nominated attorney general of the United States, at a Senate confirmation hearing after she admitted that she had hired an illegal alien to take care of her child and had failed to pay taxes on time. Nannygate, as the media dubbed it, required Zoe Baird to withdraw her name.

We talked about the foul odor in today's political air. Grandpa Sidney pulled a book from a shelf. He fingered the pages and then read me a poem.

"I Know Something Good about You"
By Louis C. Shimon

Wouldn't this old world be better?
If folks we met would say,
"I know something good about you,"
And treat us just that way?

Wouldn't it be fine and dandy,
If each handclasp, fond and true,
Carried with it assurance,
"I know something good about you!"

Wouldn't life be lots more happy,
If the good that is in us all
Were the only things about us
That folks bothered to recall?

Wouldn't life be lots more happy,
If we praised the good we see?
For there's such a lot of goodness,
In the worst of you and me.

Wouldn't it be nice to practice
That fine way of thinking too?
You know something good about me,
I know something good about you.

"Did you like it?" he asked.
I did.
"Let me read you another one," he said.

"Happiness"
By Priscilla Leonard

Happiness is like a crystal,
Fair and exquisite and clear,
Broken in a million pieces,
Shattered, scattered, far and near,
Now and then along life's pathway,
Lo! Some shining fragments fall,
But there are so many pieces,
No one ever finds them all.

My father, Grandpa Sidney, had through his lens rudely awakened me to the conflicts that the people in the United States – and I – were facing.

COMING OUT WITH CLINTON

A few months before the 1992 election, a "shocking" news article revealed there were gay bars at Camp Lejeune, a marine base in North Carolina. That gays were serving in the armed forces burst out of the closet! Surprise, surprise. Clinton had to take a position to end the ban on homosexuals serving in the military, which the Bush camp hoped would cost him votes. Gays had served in the military for years under a "don't ask, don't tell" policy. Upon declaring that one was homosexual, a discharge was processed. Nevertheless, the greater majority of the American people were under the impression that there were no gays in the military.

The arguments to keep gays out echoed the pleas to keep blacks from serving in World War II. How could blacks and whites live together? They couldn't sit on a bus together. They couldn't drink from the same water fountain or go to the same restroom.

Now, how could a heterosexual live with a homosexual? Wouldn't it lead to AIDS? Wouldn't it be bad for morale? An ideal of what the armed forces "should" be was threatened. A dream of a "superman" military was shattered.

Gays began to "come out" in the military. The military and the country panicked, terrified by something it didn't understand. In Canada and in Israel, where gays fought bravely, it was no big deal. It was difficult for the military and the country to understand gay sexual behavior, even as gays, who had served honorably, explained their sexuality in a nonthreatening manner.

When I was a teenager, homosexuals were often teased and called queer. Blacks were discriminated against and called niggers. Despite my own homophobia and prejudices, I tried to support, tolerate and accept others. As I got to know gays and blacks and people with different religions, I learned that we had many things in common with which to bond.

When a friend committed suicide because he was so ashamed to be gay that he could not tell anyone, even his parents, who he thought would kill themselves if he told them, I was devastated and terrified that lack of understanding led to an innocent death. I befriended and was befriended by many gays in New Hope, Pennsylvania and thought I understood what it was to be gay.

Yet, when my son was a sophomore at Yale, he came out. I panicked, cried, and tried to change him. Not only was I afraid for him because of the increased chance of his becoming infected with AIDS but also my dream of having a male heir to carry on my name evaporated. I tried to change him and suggested he get therapy. He and his friends spent hours with me, explaining their sexuality and their lack of choice. After I read books, talked to therapists, and understood that being gay was not a choice one made, I realized my folly and embraced him unconditionally with love. I thanked him for being so patient and understanding with me. I recognized the need to learn about people and things I did not understand and know how to wage a different war against my terror – using weapons of education and appreciating that earth's great treasure lies in human personality.

The gay issue lit a fire in the belly of Clinton's opposition. Less than a month after Clinton was inaugurated, Ross Perot, a multibillionaire businessman, went on television asking people to join United We Stand by contributing $15. Who were his targets? Opponents of gays in the military, people who did not want to understand, who were afraid and paralyzed with the terror of the unknown. His opposition to George Bush had garnered him more than 20 percent of the vote in 1992. Clinton was elected because Perot split right-wing voters.

If Clinton failed, Perot thought it would be President Perot in 1996.

If there was a way to promote respect for and the reality of interacting with others, would the divide-and-conquer strategy promoted and exacerbated by politicians with the aid of the media disappear?

After Bill Clinton woke up one morning to learn that the World Trade Center in New York City had been bombed and America became aware of a failure of the Bush administration, which had been lax with its immigration and naturalization policies, the issue of gays being accepted in the military disappeared from the front pages and Bill Clinton's agenda. So did gay pride marches and Ross Perot. A more violent form of terror took its place.

Scholars and diplomats commented in reaction to the World Trade Center disaster. Our jealous and envious enemies, who used the emancipation of the poor as their justification, were exposing the country's imperfections.

The terrorists were men abandoning the rule of law, just as our leaders had. Vengeance was begetting vengeance, and grudges were breeding hate.

I read Maya Angelou's "I Know Why the Caged Bird Sings." Writing magnetic metaphors, she described her growing up in the '30s and '40s, a time when African Americans were called Negroes or Darkies, a time when, though free, they were still "caged birds." Her words made me see that when a person of any kind is in captivity or "in the closet," he had to sing to survive; or else, he died spiritually, if not physically. Were our enemies those who were caged? Or those who put people in the cages?

With the coming of May in the Eastern United States comes glorious weather and perfect blue skies unblemished by clouds. A bright sun radiates warmth that comforts. The pink dogwoods, yellow forsythia, and purple lilacs add color that excites the eye. Daffodils, hyacinths, and tulips burst with life and strength. Birds sing in trees bursting with soft green leaves.

While the skies were clear and the air warm, there was a bad smell in the air left from the Reagan-Bush years. Richard Perlman, a childhood friend and business associate, informed me that I would be reading his name in the papers as a defendant in a lawsuit by the Resolution Trust Company against the directors of a bank board on which he served. In the '80s, an appointment to a bank board was an honor. In the late '70s, the savings and loans were on the verge of insolvency because the interest rate they could charge was regulated. Savings and loans were in trouble because people were withdrawing their deposits and putting them in banks where the money would earn more interest. Reagan deregulated the savings and loans, and they began to make high-interest loans to developers.

In 1986, the tax laws were changed, causing a recession and defaults on loans. As the savings and loans failed, a government agency was established. The Resolution Trust Company took over the savings and loans and began to sue the directors of the savings and loans for mismanagement! My friend cried to me, "I heard the national anthem being played, and I could not salute."

It had taken twelve years of Reagan and Bush to get the country over its head in debt. Every child that was born in 1993 owed $65,000 of the national debt!

The foul air infected Clinton too. He talked negatively, blaming the past administrations, and neglected using the bully pulpit he needed to point out positive accomplishments. He did not meet the challenge of becoming a cheerleader and picking up the morale of his fellow citizens.

His lens shifted from eliminating poverty, poor education, and understanding the value of diversity.

President Clinton lost respect due to his weakness in managing. He was seen as a man of ideas but not of implementation. While there were hopes that he would "get it together," taking over a bureaucracy as large as the federal government and making quick changes was no easy task.

Lanie Guanier's nomination as head of the civil rights section of the Department of Justice was withdrawn after Republicans challenged her for statements she made in law review articles. Why, I asked, didn't people know that professors and law students often debated controversial subjects and took positions that argue a point, even though the professor or student may not believe in the point? Her castigation by right-wingers in Congress cast a chill on academic freedom and free discourse in society.

On the surface, Americans did not have it so bad. Conveniences made life easier. Electricity, air-conditioning, cars, restaurants, television, and air travel were available to most. But mentally, living was stressful because most people were concerned about taxes, inflation, investments, earning more money than one needed, and trying to figure out the meaning and purpose of living in a convoluted world. Cultivating deep human relationships was difficult. "How-to" books filled bookstore shelves.

Elsewhere in the world, the atmosphere was churning a violent storm. As the crisis in Bosnia heated up, a friend, who was an official with the International Monetary Fund, warned that in his experience, wars made presidents popular. He expressed his fear that the United States did not understand the ethnic culture of the Serbs, Croats, and Muslims. According to his analysis, only a strongman like Marshall Tito could keep them from killing each other. "Unless one is born like them, it is difficult to be one of them," he commented, advising that the United States should stay out of their tribal fights. When I asked him about the prospects for peace in the Middle East, he observed there was a chance "only if those who want it strive harder than those who don't."

Suddenly, it seemed as though the skies cleared. It seemed that those who wanted peace wanted it more than those who didn't. The Berlin Wall fell in the fall of 1993. Israelis and Palestinians, two brutal enemies, recognized each other's existence and signed a peace treaty in Oslo, Norway.

With the seas calm, Bill Clinton pulled off the classiest move of his presidency. He invited all living presidents to the White House to recognize the Oslo accords. Former presidents Carter, Ford, and Bush accepted while Nixon and Reagan did not. By inviting the former presidents to sleep at the

White House, he got them to support NAFTA, the North American Free Trade Agreement. NAFTA, passed in November 1993, created a free trade bloc of Canada, the United States, and Mexico and became the first concrete step toward uniting the North American countries with the Latin American nations – steps to eliminate poverty in the nations to our south. Science took a leap forward with the repair of a faulty mirror of the Hubble telescope that was put in orbit in 1990. Endeavor, a rescue rocket, took corrective lenses 367 miles above the earth in order to permit scientists to see views of space never seen before.

As 1993 ended, President Clinton gained popularity and confidence. The United States was clearly the strongest world power. Fortunately, Clinton did not view the United States as a superpower that could dictate events. Terror seemed to dissipate with understanding. I breathed a sigh of relief.

PULP POLITICS

At the dawn of 1994, when Clinton took steps to become stronger, Senators Robert Dole and Philip Gramm and Congressman Newt Gingrich captured the airwaves, spearheading an ugly display, attempting to expose an allegedly poor investment made fourteen years before Clinton became president. Called Whitewater to remind people of Watergate, the scandal that brought Richard Nixon to his resignation, Whitewater reared the ugly heads of partisanship and manipulation.

Conservatives in the United States switched strategies and began to appeal to the masses by simplifying problems that had difficult solutions. They promoted tax cuts, more benefits, more prisons, and more roads – more of everything with less money. Anti-Semitism rose among ultraconservative whites and, scarier yet, in the black community. Louis Farrakhan appealed to poverty-level blacks and lashed out at "Jewish impostors." Who would have thought that the people the Jewish people marched for would be their enemy?

As Adolph Hitler taught, there is an irony when the helpless are desperate.

Schindler's List, a movie about a Polish businessman, Oskar Schindler, who harbored Jews in Krakow, Poland, made audiences cry and realize that the Holocaust could happen again.

In early March, CBS television commentator Dan Rather showed a press conference with Clinton and Eduard Shevardnadze, the former foreign minister of the Soviet Union, now the president of Georgia. The United States announced it had given twenty billion dollars in aid to Georgia. The news conference turned to the question-and-answer period. Questions were fired about the alleged unethical behavior of Hillary Clinton. Clinton, pointing his finger at the questioner, defended his wife, saying that he did not know anyone with a better sense of right and wrong than Hillary and that if everyone had her sense of right and wrong, the world would be better off.

It was almost impossible to develop a positive, enthusiastic visionary and trustworthy leader. Why? Because the omniscience of the media discouraged almost all but the avaricious to devote their talent and energy to public service, where one was exposed to the kind of public scrutiny that was in vogue. Television was so instantaneous in reporting events that it shaped policies. The politician was no longer the creator of the agenda. The thirty-second sound bite was in charge.

Sports took on the symbol of pageantry. The New York Rangers won the Stanley Cup for the first time since 1940, and New York treated the victory like the First Coming. World Cup soccer filled stadiums to capacity. Sports figures, like rock stars, let the people vent their aggression.

In the Name of the Father was a popular movie about five people who were framed by the British police to take the blame for an Irish Republican Army bombing that killed many people in a pub. After fifteen years, they were freed when a lawyer suppressed evidence that vindicated them.

Television sound bites, movies, and sports were now the lenses through which people saw the world in which they lived. They had the power to terrorize and to promote misunderstanding. What images the media lens captured mattered.

A FAMILY AFFAIR

Searching for values that were truly valid in the world of 1995 was frustrating. Basic ethics as set forth in the Ten Commandments or in Leviticus, chapter 19, while truly great, were not practical in a world as aggressive as it was at almost all levels of society.

A poem by an anonymous writer told the story:

> Friends, Americans, my countrymen, lend me your ear,
> I come not to bury the politicians of the right,
> But to praise them for their willingness to fight,
> But lest they forget the faces of the white,
> And black, and yellow have fallen into pools of blood,
> Fighting for freedom and holding back the flood,
> Of Fascism, Nazism, and Communism.
>
> Now it is the time to say, "Power to those who have the water,"
> Such a motto cannot but lead to slaughter,
> The cries of freedom's dying sons,
> The wails of those sons' mothers,
> Will cause those deaths to be in vain,
> The victories worth nil – and lost not won.
>
> Remember Abe – who said – A house divided cannot stand,
> Now is a time to call on all to march,
> Not apart – but hand in hand,
> Now is not the time to budget cut at the expense of the poor,
> Because twenty years ago we spent our savings on the Vietnam War,
> We've helped our enemies rebuild,
> Now is not the time for babies in the ghetto to be killed.

No, now is not the time to take away freedom and opportunity for
    those among us
Less able,
Not the time to hurt so we can save the dollar,
If we do we will be certain to hear the injured holler,
And end up with a society less stable.

No, now is not the time to forget this country was born to raise
    freedom for all,
Joining together, caring for all – that is the only way the child
Freedom can grow To be Liberty and Justice – tall – and for all.

So stop the drums, stop the fife – of the Contract for America,
It is not the music of life – but of strife,
For now forget the fate of the Almighty Buck,
Let's join our hands and work together for Lady Luck,
So that when the tides change – the political right will hear the
opposing
Generals yell, "Power to those who have the water."

Newt Gingrich, the Republican leader in the House of Representatives, called for a return to family values. What were family values? What was it that the family was to care about? Were Americans being called upon to respect elders, honor teachers, and get offspring a good education? Or were they being asked to be caged in a rigid system again? Was the conservatism of 1995 just another way for those who had been out of power to increase their power? Just as there were few liberals in the early part of the twentieth century, there were few vocal conservatives in the early '70s. By 1995, conservatives had become vocal. Significantly, they were persuasive because they exposed improprieties committed by Democratic legislators who had been in power far too long in Congress. More problems festered as Congress cut needed programs for the poor, reduced spending, and cut taxes. Instead of helping the poor, the Republicans, who contracted with America, favored the rich. Would fear be at its abyss and lead to a zenith of greed?

The poor were mind-boggled. Used to hearing no evil and seeing no evil on the theory that you don't know what you don't see, television brought the world to them. Sensing a split between black and white and solidarity among blacks and poor, Louis Farrakhan led a million-man march in Washington. Would Farrakhan be like Ross Perot's run for the presidency, a flash in the pan? A symptom of worsening underlying problems, Farrakhan's march terrorized many.

Unfortunately, the middle class was a majority beset by fear, trembling, and anger. The middle class walked a tight rope between the American dream and economic disaster. Companies to which they had been loyal were laying off people from good jobs. Downsizing, as it was called, was supposedly going to make the United States more efficient and competitive in a world that was going global.

Unions did not protect their members against foreign competition. The college graduates, who were laid off from middle – and upper-management positions, had said, "Who needs unions?" They thought that security was there for them since they had done the right things. They had gone to college and had worked hard. That formula for success failed so many.

I recalled the day in 1967 when I sat with Abigail Pollak, a childhood friend, at the Mohawk Canoe Club on the Delaware River in Trenton, New Jersey. A sophomore at Dartmouth College, I had read Floyd Hunter's book *Community Power Structure* in which the author wrote that all social relationships were political relationships – that political power was determined by the ability to influence men's minds. What I saw through my lens was that money was power since money permitted one to influence his or her own mind.

A glance at history reaffirmed that the upper classes try to keep people down, either actively or passively, even though they talked a good game of trying to help. When push came to shove, they tried to keep themselves above the rest. The only way the lower classes rose was by their own guts and organization, which was hard to do, or by the upper classes falling due to greed and laziness.

As spring buds sprouted on the tree limbs and the green leaves followed yellow forsythia, crocuses burst through the earth and daffodils joined them soon thereafter. *Forrest Gump*, a retarded loser who becomes a winner, swept most of the Academy Awards!

Americans, as a family, were hoping to be winners too.

A real winner, O. J. Simpson, one of America's greatest football stars, was charged with the murder of his wife. The sports idol led the police in

Los Angeles on a fifty-mile chase, which was televised nationally. As his trial began, I vented my feelings and penned a poem.

> Guilty or not – Americans ask,
> As the prosecutors tediously complete the task,
> To show O.J. murdered two,
> So he will get the justice due.
>
> An American hero reduced to zero,
> Is not part of American culture,
> How can O.J. spend his life behind bars?
>
> Will the jury vent the fury?
> Will society be scared if O.J.'s spared?
> Will there be reasonable doubt,
> So from his crime O.J. will get out?
>
> They call Cochran, Shapiro, and Bailey the Dream Team,
> Lawyers who have the ability to scheme,
> To twist and turn the facts,
> To prove that the evidence is what the prosecutor lacks.

The verdict came. O.J. was not guilty.

What did the verdict do to the country? Had it created even more of a split between whites and blacks? Would it make police more careful? Would it reduce respect for the criminal justice system?

The blunders began the night of the murder – the crime scene had not been properly secured – and the policeman who went over a wall after seeing blood on O.J.'s Ford Bronco testified he did it to protect O.J. His lie was obvious. Not only had he scaled the fence in question but also he had left the Bronco on an open lot where anyone could have tampered with it. A coroner did not examine the bodies for ten hours and then did not keep the stomach contents. O.J.'s blood was carried around by another policeman and was not properly stored. The list of errors went on and on.

Then, an American citizen, Timothy McVeigh, a white supremacist, bombed a federal building to avenge the FBI's actions against a religious cultist, a Branch Davidian. The shock of seeing a building collapse with men, women, and children losing their lives sent shockwaves through the country.

On April 19, 1995, when Timothy McVeigh killed hundreds of innocents, the United States had a tiny minority of only two hundred fifty thousand people who had assets over $5,000,000. A mere 1 percent! For them, wealth was a wall protecting them from social instability, a wall that was both a reaction to the moral chaos of inequality and dependence on it.

I had an opportunity to go to Oaxaca, Mexico, to learn Spanish. While there, I visited the ancient city of Mitla, once capital of Zapotec and Mayan civilizations that had all but disappeared. Once rich, they fell to materialism, raping of the land, deforesting of mountains that caused erosion, and polluting of streams. I asked myself whether there was a cycle of growth, destruction of nature, and then a decline of a civilization. Could the past be looked at to predict the future? Would the global economy raise the standard of living of all? Would the crime of poverty disappear?

What would happen, I asked, if CNN played an upbeat tone and was available for the world's family to see?

TICKING TIME BOMBS OR
SHAKEN AND STIRRED

Snow covered the ground on New Year's morning, 1996. A goose gawked beneath a gray sky. Loneliness and fear filled the air; people did not know what to say to one another.

Republicans engaged in a bitter primary campaign with Robert Dole, the front-runner, pitted against Steve Forbes, a multibillionaire, who, while expounding a flat tax, spent twenty-five million of his own dollars causing havoc in the Republican ranks. Pat Buchanan, a right-winger, and Lamar Alexander, a moderate Tennessee Republican, joined the fray. The Senate majority pilloried Hillary Clinton over Whitewater.

President Clinton and the Congress performed a fire dance around the national budget, sexual equality, gays in the military, welfare, and medical reform.

The first primary election in New Hampshire was chaotic. Pat Buchanan won by 1 percent over Bob Dole. Lamar Alexander got 23 percent, and Steve Forbes garnered 12 percent. The vote represented the American electorate. A perception pervaded that politics was divisive.

Religious conservatives and dissatisfied workers made up 25 percent of the population. Twenty-five percent were establishment, 23 percent were moderates, and 12 percent wanted less tax and wanted to rid themselves of the Internal Revenue Service. Ten percent did not know what they wanted.

Senator Bob Dole picked former congressman and football star Jack Kemp to be his running mate. Bob Dole turned out to be a very uninspiring candidate. The presidential campaign in the United States took on a drone of boredom. During the debates with Clinton, Dole avoided answering questions posed to him by newsman Jim Lehrer, ending each answer with a question for President Clinton.

ALBERT M. STARK ✖ 38

The reelection of Bill Clinton revealed that the American people were basically satisfied to be in the hands of a clever, cunning, not-so-honest president and a ruthless, mean-spirited Congress with a slight Republican majority. The public viewed the president as a well-meaning thief and the Congress as the cop watching so that the cookie jar was not robbed.

Election night was a contrast between the old and the new. Dole gave a sad, rambling thank-you speech and ended on a bitter note, saying, "I'm going to sit back for a few days and then stand up for what I think is right." He was still running.

Clinton, on the other hand, played his victory like it was a coronation. The old statehouse, an old antebellum mansion in Little Rock, Arkansas, was lit brightly. Trees in front of the house were wired with bulbs like a Christmas tree would be. Thousands of supporters gathered in front of a stage that was constructed on the front lawn.

An African American opera singer warmed up the crowd singing "God Bless America." An announcer proclaimed, "The president of the United States of America, William Jefferson Clinton, the First Lady, and Chelsea Clinton." The three of them came forward from a broad open doorway and strode like Miss America contestants, stiff, waving, trying to be royalty. Clinton wore a well-fitted dark suit, Hillary a soft beige dress, and Chelsea looked like she was going to a prep school prom.

Then the Gores were introduced. Al Gore was typical Gore, stiff, his face filled with a forced smile. Tipper looked like the American flag, and their daughters wore blue blazers and red skirts. Their young son was Mr. Brooks Brothers, Jr. The hilarious scene was supposed to be presidential.

Gore gave a speech, his kickoff speech for president in 2000, then introduced Clinton, praising him, Hillary, and their record. Clinton followed with a well-written address. Most of what he said was rhetoric. I sadly watched the best America had to offer.

Across the oceans, violence broke out in England again as the peace process between the Irish Republican Army and England broke down with the bombing of a London office building.

Israel repressed the Arabs. Arabs killed Israelis. War followed in some form or another. The winner repressed the loser. The repression caused terrorism. More repression followed with retaliatory attacks and more terrorist activity. Repression cost the winner dearly. Peace efforts made by winners to moderates began, followed by acts to destroy the peace process by extremists. Moderates, who won concessions, wanted to engage in more of the peace process. Extremists, who felt left out, sabotaged the peace process.

Israel's killing innocent citizens in Tyre horrified me. The motivation to attack was inspired by an upcoming election. How sad it was that politics played so great a role in creating wars.

The Middle East was a tinderbox. Out of nowhere, the Turkish prime minister called on Saddam Hussein to control the Kurds who were backing terrorism by Iran. The moderates and extremists in almost all of the Middle Eastern nations were battling each other. The Israeli situation became more and more precarious. More and more Israelis and Palestinians were killed. Israel lit a fuse when it declared it was going to close a tunnel beneath the Temple Mount. To see so much hatred developing between people who were neighbors was disheartening.

A cycle of violence was the story of the day.

World events made me feel like I was in the middle of a storm, being battered around and out of control. CNN told its worldwide audience that the peacemaker Rabin was defeated by the warrior Netanyahu in Israel, that World War III was about to break out. When Boris Yeltsin, a bright light in an oppressive world, became ill and canceled a meeting with Vice President Al Gore, the world shook because Yeltsin was ill.

Even the uplifting mood of the Olympics was shattered by the crash of TWA Flight 800, which was rumored to have been blown up by terrorists on its way from New York to Paris. Newscasts punctuated with the triumph of the human spirit at Atlanta were interrupted by the salvage and search operation in the Atlantic Ocean off Long Island.

The TWA investigation became more and more confusing. One day it was a crash caused by terrorists, the next it was caused by mechanical failure in the plane itself. A bomb exploded in a plaza in Atlanta; and in a rush to get the culprit, a security guard was arrested then released.

People did not know what to or who to believe. Neither did I.

CLINTON CONFIDENTIAL

An African American singer, a Jewish female justice, and an evangelist set the tone for his second term. Jessye Norman, cloaked in crimson, sang an American medley of "God Bless America," her full mane of hair waving as she blasted refrains. Ruth Bader Ginsburg became the first woman justice of the Supreme Court to swear in a president of the United States. Billy Graham gave the invocation.

In his second inaugural address, Clinton took his own ideas, the best of the Democratic platform and the best of the Republican platform and wove them together into a centrist fabric. The boy from Hope tried to sell Democratic ideals inculcated in the party's platform for over fifty years. Tired of the "L" word, a brand as scorned as the scarlet "A" at the time of the Salem witches, Clinton abandoned liberal principles.

He spoke about the twentieth century and about building a bridge to the twenty-first. Sermonizing, he painted utopia with a broad brush. In his "land of new promises," Eden would be created. Polite applause echoed skepticism. Was his speech a wish or promise?

Madeline Albright became the first female secretary of state. As spring arrived in 1997, one thousand days remained until the millennium. The Dow Jones Industrial Average had reached 7,000.

A sense of relief spread across the country when, in early June, a jury found Timothy McVeigh guilty and sentenced him to death. A leap of faith infused the justice system. The stock market jumped to 7,400.

The burgeoning "computer industry," the Chicago Bulls basketball team, and Tiger Woods, a young golf phenomenon, dominated the headlines. The United States was on a roll.

On a magnificent Indian summer day, I sat on a boat in the middle of the Delaware River and read a book written by Howell Raines, *Fly Fishing through the Midlife Crisis.* An observation caught my attention. "The stability of American society depends less on defending the rich against imaginary threats than in providing a decent standard of living for the unfortunate."

My study of Roman history in college had taught me that there are many styles of leadership, that the strength of the Romans and their alliances broke down when the society became so wealthy and satisfied that it did not change the structure from the agrarian-expansionist beginnings to one of betterment of all. The Roman Empire failed when it did not break down the aristocracy, but instead did all it could to preserve and protect it. I filled up with an air of optimism, thinking that Bill Clinton had learned Roman history and did not want to have it repeat itself.

I thought about my upbringing in a Jewish home. I had been reminded often that in every anti-Semitic movement, there had been a cry that the Jews killed Christ. My study of Roman history in college had also taught me that the worship of Jehovah (God) had spread through the dispersion of the Jews in the Greek period. The Maccabees'revolt against the Seleucids started a revival of religious enthusiasm and missionary activity among non-Jews. In the first century AD, the cult of Jehovah had attracted a large body of converts who regularly attacked synagogues.

In the reign of Tiberius, Jesus, a Jewish prophet, proclaimed a new message. Jesus attracted large crowds, was greeted as a miracle worker, and when he went on his prophetic mission to Jerusalem, he was welcomed as the son of King David. The Jewish high priest Caiaphas, who thought it his duty to defend orthodoxy and feared that the disturbances over Jesus would be thought by the Roman governors of Judea to be a rebellion, got Pontius Pilate, the procurator, to sentence Jesus to crucifixion, the sentence for rioting or rebellion. At the time of the crucifixion, Jesus got little attention; but his disciples, believing Jesus was resurrected, kept his message alive and set up a sect distinct from the Jewish religion and carried Jesus's message throughout Asia Minor, Greece, and Rome. Paul, a convert, laid the foundations of a universal Christian church with his visits and letters.

By the middle of the first century, Christians were plentiful. Christ was killed in AD 33. Christians, like Jews, have been persecuted. Why? They were not content to share the world with other worshipers. They aimed to abolish them altogether. Those who wished to live and let live in matters of religion resented the attack on Roman gods. Neither Jews nor Christians escaped by being aloof from society. In an essentially sociable community, self-isolation was disliked and suspected.

The teaching of Jesus was set down in written records of the four Gospels, dated AD 65 to AD 100, and became accepted as authoritative. That, with other writings, became the New Testament.

I wondered whether those lessons taught by the Romans would also not be forgotten. If that were so, we were heading for a century of peace and tranquility.

By coincidence or fate, a religious puzzle spread through the Internet. It was called the JIGSAW puzzle: Jews, Islamics, Gentiles Spiritually Attached Worldwide.

The puzzle solution asked, "Wouldn't it be phenomenal if religious causes preaching superiority, which led to prejudice, were abolished by mutual understanding?" To do that, one had to engender respect for others' beliefs and not say, "My way is the only way."

Little did I know that a mere four years later the lessons taught by the Romans, Christians and Jews would be forgotten.

EMBARRASSED TO BE AN AMERICAN

In 1998, *Focus*, a book by Albert Ries, presented the argument that the future would require more and more specialization and less and less conglomeration, diversification, and convergence. His theory required focus. Ries analogized with the sun and the laser, arguing that the sun had enormous energy, which it spread out over the earth, burning only a few who exposed themselves too much. The laser, a low-energy beam, could focus its energy to make a great imprint. Espousing laserlike behavior for leaders, he wrote that leaders had to foresee the future and jump with both feet into it, putting all of one's eggs in one basket. "See the future and it is yours," he said.

Cars buzzed along the freeways along with a proliferation of SUVs, large, oversized cars, and vans on truck bodies. Had Americans forgotten about the oil crisis twenty-five years before which drew it to smaller, more efficient cars? Was the United States going to be more and more dependent on foreign oil? Suffering, high interest rates, and recession followed the wild 1960s, with its gas-guzzlers. How would the party end this time?

Then 1998 brought us the Clinton sex scandal with Monica Lewinsky. The scandal took on a life of its own and became a scandal not just of the president but also of the press and prosecutor. To divert focus, Clinton created a crisis with Iraq which almost brought the United States to war. At the last minute, Saddam Hussein agreed to weapons inspections. Meanwhile, the United States spent billions to move ships and airplanes.

The pressure on Bill Clinton had built to the point where he had to admit to an inappropriate relationship with a twenty-two-year-old.

Ken Starr, the Whitewater prosecutor, delivered the Ken Starr Report to Congress in full view of CNN cameras. Networks began showing President Clinton's testimony before a grand jury, and many speculated his presidency was near its end. The House of Representatives voted to begin impeachment proceedings against President Clinton. Four articles of impeachment were released for lying about private sex. Yet, while the

Republicans were sticking him like a pig with a hot poker, Clinton was at the United Nations speaking about a war on terrorism.

Clinton, in the midst of the fray, went to the West Bank to seek peace and create his legacy.

To further switch the focus from his improprieties, missiles attacked terrorist camps in Sudan and Afghanistan. Seventy-five cruise missiles worth one million dollars apiece were fired at an individual, Osama bin Laden, not at a country.

For the first time, the United States was at war against an individual, not a nation. The world had not only superpowers and supermarkets but now also superpeople.

Bin Laden retaliated with an attack on the USS Cole and on embassies abroad. An escalating religious war, a war between two civilizations, between the rich and the poor, had begun; and I wondered to myself where it would end.

Reading the newspapers was a horror. The United States was using terrorist tactics against Muslims bent on destroying the United States. Would civil rights be a thing of the past in a few years?

Who were the terrorists? Muslims, the media proclaimed.

I imagined how angry a Muslim felt when he walked into a mosque in Cordoba, Spain, seeing the desecration and the transformation of a holy Muslim place to a Christian cathedral. Wouldn't it be the same feeling a Jew had when the Wailing Wall in Jerusalem was under Muslim control? Or how Judah Maccabee felt when he found idols in a synagogue?

There was a war going on where the aristocracy was trying to bespeak a moral superiority to protect itself and put down all others that did not agree with them. Was this not the same cleansing philosophy of Queen Isabella in the Inquisition and Hitler with the Holocaust?

Helmut Kohl lost his bid for reelection as prime minister in Germany. For the first time in years, Social Democrats rose to power.

Unfortunately, there was no one strong leader in the Western world who had the respect of people.

War was imminent in Yugoslavia. Little folks were being left by the wayside. The '90s were beginning to be called the years of greed. The Clintons, labeled "corrupt world leaders," and "ugly Western society" were the subject of story after story. People in other parts of the world, suffering on subsistence wages, were seeing CNN's portrayal of an aristocracy they did not like or respect. They saw politicians who were selfish, to whom the public be damned, leaving room for pedagogues to create extremism that was destructive to well-meaning people who lived in Western societies.

Why could not multiculturalism exist side by side?

I saw my Jewish heritage as an opportunity to understand the suffering of others and wanted to learn more about why the establishment did not see the long-term value of lifting up the poor who, if not lifted up, would be the source of their destruction.

The mansions of Newport, Rhode Island, were now museums. No family had been able to maintain its wealth and prominence forever. The Alhambra in Spain was a tourist attraction, a symbol of something bigger than life, but, in reality, an example of how the need for defense and protection from warring factions led to control of, discipline of, and exploitation of the populous.

Was it a timeless truth that the populace craved and yearned for leadership? When could a leader be courageous enough to know his limits? The events of the day sparked these questions in my mind.

In December 1998, I had the opportunity to visit North Vietnam. A woman in her mid-thirties told me, "My father went to war. I was about two years old. My brother was six. One night we left our home in Hanoi about midnight. My mother loaded what we had on a bicycle. My brother pushed another. My mother was carrying me. We walked and walked in the dark. One of the bicycles broke. We went into the countryside to live. My brother went to school in tunnels. My father was lucky. He wasn't killed. He came home after four years. He worked for the government. We had rations. We were very poor. Since 1990, with the open market, things are better now." She pointed to two boys. "Those boys make about $12 a month. They work six days a week from morning until dark."

I had been in the jungles of Laos with its bomb craters two years before, where I hiked up a rocky trail that still showed signs of Agent Orange's destruction and wondered how an American infantryman could have survived in the environment. I was sad for the 3.5 to 5 million Vietnamese who were killed in ten years of fighting, but even more pathetically sorry for the Vietnam veterans and the families of fifty thousand young Americans who would have been my age if they had not lost their lives. I had been too embarrassed to call myself an American.

How, I asked myself, could intelligent men send B52's laden with napalm and helicopters with machine guns to burn and shoot those brave souls who could not read or write and who had not traveled more than thirty miles from their birthplaces? How could the United States talk about human rights when, in reality, one human error after another made by men who did not or would not understand escalated a needless, useless war? Richard

Nixon, John F. Kennedy, and Lyndon Johnson had never been to Vietnam. George H. W. Bush had never been to Iran or Iraq. Bill Clinton had never been to Hanoi, North Korea, or Baghdad.

Was that the problem? The leader had never met the "enemy." Worse yet, he didn't try to understand them.

HARBORING HUMAN NATURE

The end of a millennium causes people to look back and into the future. Despite Clinton's prblems, as 1999 began, the United States economy appeared to be moving along well. The countries of Europe and the Far East were recovering. Stock markets throughout the world closed at record levels. New technology was making worldwide communication easier. China was admitted to the World Trade Organization and was becoming the new factory of the twenty-first century. Japan's economy was reviving.

Great Greek writers said that life and death are of equal importance because to appreciate life, it is necessary to face death, that to fall into the darkness is to appreciate shadows, which one can follow to the light. With its many discoveries, the twentieth century had been a marvel. Discoveries were being made about solar neutrinos. Gnomics was being born in molecular science. The Internet was in its infancy.

At the political conventions in August, the Democrats nominated Al Gore and a Connecticut senator, Joseph Lieberman. George W. Bush and Dick Cheney would carry the Republican banner. Feeding on Clinton's unpopularity, Bush had a fifteen-point lead in the polls. The rich were getting richer faster than at any time since the Industrial Revolution in the latter part of the nineteenth century. The high-tech revolution was mind-boggling. So much change, so much progress. Yet the changes required keeping up with the changes. Poor and those who stayed static fell behind.

Bush and Cheney moved further and further to the right, splintering the country between the rich and poor.

The issues facing the country deeply divided it. Christian whites were against blacks and Hispanics; the rich were battling the poor, and the right was against the left.

On election night, the television commentators predicted Gore to be the winner. Shortly after 9:00 p.m., they retracted their prognostication because there was a foul-up in the voting in Florida. A ballot was confusing; and Pat Buchanan, running as an Independent, garnered votes that were intended for Gore. The Green Party, led by Ralph Nader, had taken away votes that would have continued the Clinton years.

The stock market fell and the media blamed it on the election but in reality, business was slowing. The country was polarized with the heartland having voted for Bush and the populated states going for Gore.

Not only was the election a virtual tie but the Congress was split. With gridlock, nothing would get done.

The United States was at a great divide. Democracy was challenged to its limits. Muslims were becoming more violent.

At the end of November, the election was still being contested. Al Gore had won the popular vote by five hundred thousand. Bush was winning by seven hundred thirty votes, less than .001 of 1 percent. The courts were involved. The imperfections of the voting system were in full view.

On December 13, 2000, the Supreme Court decided against Al Gore in a divisive, obtuse decision. Al Gore conceded. Bush accepted the presidency, speaking about his campaign promises, tax cuts for the wealthy. He said nothing about technological advances, environmental advances, or fuel cell cars to reduce the need for foreign oil. He began to appoint right-wing cabinet secretaries.

There were lessons that had to be learned from the 2000 election. The Constitution had to be amended to move the election to the second weekend in September, and all the polls should close at the same time countrywide. The Electoral College had to be kept, but "winner takes all" provisions had to be changed so that each congressional district had a representative. Campaigning had to be limited to a period from March to September. All election districts should use the same machines.

Whether the lessons would be learned would remain to be seen. The challenges were there to be tackled.

Companies failed, and fear took over from greed.

Slobodan Milosevich resigned as the president of Yugoslavia. He had lost the election and then canceled the results. Protesters stormed the Parliament in Belgrade, calling him a war criminal for the ethnic cleansing he led against Muslims in Bosnia and Herzegovina.

Middle East peace was elusive, and the war between the Palestinians and the Israelis escalated. Vengeance begat vengeance, and grudges bred hate.

I woke up early on the morning of December 31, 1999, to see the beginning of a new millennium. On television, before Millennium Island, east of Hawaii, celebrated with native Micronesian dancers, the news featured two stories: the resignation of Boris Yeltsin as the leader in Russia and the release of three rebels in India in exchange for the release of one hundred sixty hostages held on an Air India plane in Afghanistan for a week.

What a way for a century to end and another to begin! The leader of a superpower had become powerless. A government had ceded to the criminality of terrorists.

Celebrations continued in New Zealand, Australia, Japan, China, then Europe. Finally, it was New Year's Day for me.

Nuclear arms were spreading and were becoming a threat to man's survival on earth itself. In a nuclear war, the foe would be the earth itself. People did not realize that the air, the wind, and the water would be turned to poison. Wind would spread flames. Smoke would rise and shut out the sun. With darkness and no daylight, interminable night would cause temperatures to drop below freezing. In a nuclear winter, water would turn to ice. Radioactive fallout would seep through the earth, and ground water would be contaminated. Most living things would die.

Man lived a moment away from disaster.

If Machiavellian behavior is a natural thing, to control was becoming harder and more complex.

REPUBLICAN REVULSION
(AKA THE BUSH YEARS)

On January 20, 2001, George W. Bush became the forty-third president of the United States. Money and the religious right were in power. Bill Clinton ended his term of office on a low note. He sold pardons on the final night of his presidency. Had capitalism possibly reached its apex and headed to failure due to its inability to give life, liberty, and the pursuit of happiness to people who were created equal? Would the United States suffer the destruction of the American dream? Would Bush and Cheney do what the Romans did – protect the aristocracy at the expense of the populous and spread its legions too thin? Would promised tax cuts to the rich erode the surplus that had been built up during the past eight years?

Bush got off to a good start, efficiency wise. Dick Cheney was a vice president who had no ambition to become president. His only agenda was to assist Bush. Cheney shepherded Republican legislators while Bush wooed the Democrats. The Federal Reserve Board cooperated, lowering interest rates.

Bush and Cheney quickly became the epitome of arrogance, and, worse yet, hypocrisy. Bush, rather than trying to build bridges, was inflexible, making his leadership style one of "my way or the highway."

He delivered a speech at Yale University and told the C students that they too could be presidents, alluding to his own poor academic performance. At the Naval Academy graduation, he was photographed proudly giving a diploma to the "anchor man," the bottom man in the class.

Cheney, who criticized Al Gore for making calls for political contributions from the White House, had a gathering at his residence for oil, gas, and financial barons. While no money was solicited, every attendee had recently given $100,000 or more.

Bush did everything in his power to bully people. A senator from Vermont, James Jeffords, had enough and left the Republican Party, thereby casting the balance of power in the Senate to the Democrats. He behaved similarly toward foreign nations.

Globally, it did not take Bush long to go after Saddam Hussein, who had been let out of a corner by his father, George H. W. Bush, after the Gulf War. In mid-February 2001, Bush bombed "strategic" targets outside of Baghdad.

A scene in Cormac McCarthy's *Blood Meridian* came to mind. A horrific but compelling book, it dealt with man's cruelty to man. "The good book says that he who lives by the sword perishes by the sword," Irving said.

"Who would have it any other way?" the judge asked.

"The good book does indeed count war as evil," said Irving. "Yet there's many a bloody tale of war inside it."

"It makes no difference what men think of war," the judge said. "War endures. As well, ask men what they think of stone. War was always here. Before man was here, war waited for him. The ultimate trade awaits its ultimate practitioner. That's the way it was and will be.

"It endures because young men love it and old men love it in them. Men are born for games. Nothing else. Every child knows that play is nobler than work. He knows too that the worth or merit of the game is not inherent in the game itself but rather in the value of that which is put to hazard. Games of chance require a wager to have meaning at all. Games of sport involve the skill and strength of the opponents and the humiliation of defeat and the pride of victory.

"War is the truest form of divination. It is the testing of one's will and the will of another within that larger will which, because it bends them, they are therefore forced to select. War is the ultimate game because war is at least a forcing of the unity of existence. War is God."

Was Bush, who had declared that God had told him he should be president, playing God? Was Bush war? Did he see through his lens that what joined men together was the sharing of bread? Or was it the sharing of enemies? I shuddered after I read a column in the *New York Times* on June 26, 2001 by one of my favorite columnists, Thomas Friedman. The article was entitled "A Memo from Osama."

To: All field operatives
From: Osama bin Laden

"My men: This is a great day! Did you see what we accomplished this week? We drove the U.S. Armed Forces out of three Arab countries by just threatening to hit them. I had some of our boys discuss an attack against the U.S. over cell phones. The CIA picked it up, and look what happened: the FBI team in Yemen, which was investigating the destruction of the USS Cole in Aden Harbor, just packed up and left – even though the State Department was begging them to stay. See ya. Then, after we made a few more phone calls, hundreds of U.S. – marines! – who were conducting a joint exercise with the Jordanian Army cut short their operation, got back on their amphibious vessels, and fled Jordan on Saturday. See ya. Then all the U.S. warships in Bahrain, which is the headquarters of the U.S. Fifth Fleet, were so scared of being hit by us they evacuated Bahrain's harbor and sailed out into the Persian Gulf. Boys, there is a military term for all this; it is called a "retreat." Allahu Akbar! God is great!

This is a superpower? The Americans turned tail as soon as they picked up a few threats from us. The U.S. press barely reported it, the White House press didn't even ask the president about it. But trust me, everyone out here noticed it. It told them many things: the Americans are afraid of sustaining even one casualty to their soldiers; they don't trust their own intelligence or weak Arab allies to protect them, and they have no military answer for our threat.

I love America. The Bush people want to spend $100 billion on a missile defense shield to deal with a threat that doesn't yet exist, and they run away from the threat that already exists. They think we rogues are going to attack them with intercontinental ballistic missiles with a return address on it. Are they kidding? AM I wearing a sign that says STUPID on it? We'll use layers of local operatives who can't be traced to any country . . . But the great thing is that Donald Rumsfeld is so obsessed with getting his missile-shield toy, he's been telling everyone that deterrence doesn't work anymore against people like us. So they need a missile shield instead. And Bush just repeats it. I love it . . . . So I hope the Americans invest their entire defense budget in a Star Wars shield that will have no effect on us, but will divert them from the real means and the real deterrence that could hurt us.

> Yo, Rummy, who needs missiles? We just drove the FBI, the
> Marines and the U.S. Navy out of the Middle East, with a few threats
> over Nokia cell phones! So who's the dummy, Rummy?
> God is Great, America is stupid. Revolution until victory.
>
> Osama@jihadonline (JOL)

Bush, who ran almost as an isolationist, flew all over the world to divert attention from the falling economy at home, the economy that had caused his father to be defeated by Bill Clinton. He isolated the United States in the world community, hurting the economy even more. He had lost control of his agenda by July 2001.

John Adams, the second president of the United States, said that a society that neglected to educate its poor could not survive as a democracy and planted the seeds of revolution and oligarchy. Had Bush failed to learn that lesson?

When I looked out of the window of the jetliner that sharked through clouds and entered airspace lit by a moon, I was looking forward to a pleasant two weeks paddling through a valley of grapes during harvest time.

On September 21, in the aftermath of the tragedy, I wrote in my journal, trying to figure out what happened. "The Russians had attacked Afghanistan in the late 1970s. The United States replied by helping to thwart the Russians. The CIA worked with Osama bin Laden.

The Gulf War in 1992 brought with its victory a feeling of relief. Bill Clinton was elected in November, even though George H. W. Bush had an approval rating of 92 percent in May 1992. The World Trade Center was bombed in 1993. The culprits, Muslim fundamentalists, were caught. Americans cheered and were proud of their FBI. The Saudi princes continued their old ways. American embassies were bombed. Then the USS Cole was destroyed. The stock market soared. No one listened to the cry "Poverty is a crime."

Did George W. Bush, declaring war on terrorism, make a moral and political mistake? An honest, courageous president would have said we have to begin a war on poverty. He would have stripped Osama bin Laden of his most formidable weapon: his appeal to the poor and to the fundamentalists who felt left out.

After returning from Portugal in late September 2001, I went by train to New York. Arriving in New York, I had a sense of wariness as I climbed the stairs to the main waiting room. To think that it was a logical target for a terrorist was creepy. I walked up the stairs to a taxi stand. The thoroughfare between the station and Madison Square Garden was an armed camp, filled with police cars and barricades. The walkway to Seventh Avenue was patrolled. Seventh Avenue was filled with rush hour traffic. A few blocks away, New York appeared to be normal.

But it wasn't. There was an ever-present pall penetrating almost everyone. The memory of the attack, the effects of the trauma, a sense of despair and of uncertainty filled the air.

I called a restaurant for a reservation. Normally, a reservation would be impossible to get on short notice. I was given a reservation with no problem.

I walked to Ground Zero. As I got to Canal Street in lower Manhattan, the city slowed to a drone. There were no cars, except those permitted through security checkpoints. There were a few pedestrians. Stores were closed.

When I reached a vantage point, where the pile of rubble, four to five stories high, was visible, smoke was billowing from beneath, like a campfire covered with dirt. A crane sat upon the rubble, shoveling, ever so slowly. People clicked their cameras, stared with empty eyes, cried, and shook their heads in dismay.

I walked up streets that reminded me of no-man's-land between Checkpoint Charlie in West Berlin and Friedrichstrasse in East Berlin in 1963 after the Berlin Wall went up. The streets were empty, except for lines of trailers whose signing indicated they were headquarters for the Secret Service, New York State Police, and the NYPD.

Visiting the wreckage gave me a connection with the disaster that had not been possible on television. I saw the dust, smelled the odor of death, thought of the bodies crushed, burned, cooked – and realized they were still in there.

I passed fire stations, a museum, disaster relief supplies centers, and flowers lined up in front of fire stations and photos of the men who lost their lives posted on walls.

The magnitude of it all began to come to life.

Why? What was the answer? What was the future? What would I tell my children? Or grandchildren?

Could have feeding the poor instead of bombing and embargoing Iraq prevented what I was seeing? Would have conservation of oil with efficient cars prevented what I was seeing? The questions circled my head as I approached the lights, which broadcast the latest news on a Times Square marquee.

The reality was that the terrorists had to be dealt with. What made them tick needed to become clearer to me.

I was born in 1939 as a country was about to war against another. I survived World War II and lived through a cold war. From 1952 on, anything the Communists, meaning the Soviets, did was anti-American, not in "our national interest."

But how was the wrath of Islamic fundamentalism ignited?

While at Dartmouth College, I studied international relations and was particularly interested in the origins of the cold war. Over the years, I followed what occurred in the Middle East. In 1953, Mossadegh in Iran was attempting to install social and economic reforms. A CIA coup overturned him. The United States installed Shah Pahlavi whose feudal government was overthrown twenty-five years later by Ayatollah Khomeini. Kassem in Iraq was overthrown with the help of the United States, and a CIA-sponsored Saddam Hussein was installed. The United States supported him in fighting Iran under Khomeini.

In April 1978, a popular coup overthrew the government of Mohammed Daoud in Afghanistan. Daoud had formed an alliance with Nur Mohammed Taraki, who embarked on land reform, attacking the opium-growing feudal estates, and led the new Afghan government. Taraki went to the United Nations where he managed to raise loans for crop substitution for the poppy fields owned by fundamentalists.

Taraki tried to bear down on opium production since the fundamentalists were using their money to attack the government, which they regarded as an unwholesome incarnation of modernity since Taraki was allowing women to go to school with men and outlawed arranged marriages.

The mujahideen began to torture victims, getting money from the CIA. Taraki was removed in 1979. Hafizullah Amin, educated in the United States, a fundamentalist, took over. Fearing a fundamentalist regime, Russia invaded Afghanistan in 1979. The United States supported fundamentalist freedom fighters that were being led by Osama bin Laden, the same man who was now its enemy.

Why had he turned his wrath on his sponsor, George H. W. Bush, the head of the CIA?

After the Gulf War was over in 1992, the United States insisted on an embargo against Iraq and jettisoned bin Laden. In 1996 on CBS, Lesley Stahl was interviewing the secretary of state, Madeline Albright, who had been ambassador to the United Nations.

"We've heard that half a million children have died. I mean more than died in Hiroshima. Is the price worth it?" Stahl asked.

Albright answered, "I think this is a very hard choice, but the price we think is worth it."

I had cringed when I read Albright's answer. I was sure educated men like those who flew the airplanes into the World Trade Center towers had been reminded of those words time and time again!

What went on in the past is history. The United States as a superpower had to do two things: eradicate the terrorists and be more humane. But how? It had to stop on a dime, to stop dealing with men who thwarted social and economic reforms, even if another nation or nations promoted them.

What was great about the United States was that if I wanted to write an article or a book like this, protest, or speak out, I could. If a person in Afghanistan, especially a woman, wanted to do the same, she ran the risk of being punished or beaten. If Osama bin Laden and his followers had their way, I would no longer enjoy the freedoms I have.

For the leaders of the free world, the time after September 11 was a tough world. It was tough enough to wage the battle against terrorists. A solid front was important. Citizens had to be vigilant so as not to lose civil rights in the name of a war against terrorism. The weapons of war had to be different. Memories had to be refreshed. Priorities had to be shifted. Acknowledgment of the crime of poverty had to be made before healing could take place.

The winds of war blew. Flags waved from porches, cars, rooftops. Not many realized that the pledge to the flag had the words "liberty and justice for all." Perhaps, I thought, instead of the flag waving, people should take a few moments to read the United States Constitution and remember that the men who signed it did so after providing protections for the accused. They were the freedom fighters whom the British called terrorists.

Memories were short. Only a few months before September 11, racial profiling was being condemned on the front pages of national newspapers. Now 50 percent of Americans wanted Arabs to carry identity cards.

Yet it was a fact that the FBI was successful in catching the culprits who bombed the World Trade Center in 1993 by befriending Muslims in the Jersey City area who were moderate and loved the opportunities the United States had afforded them. To profile Arabs and Muslims would be a fatal era, not only in the United States but also around the world.

The newspapers featured stories about how the business of security firms was booming and how the wealthy were hiring bodyguards and chartering private planes instead of flying on commercial airliners.

Paying for one's own protection was a sad prelude of what might be coming.

It was a time for the wealthy to speak out, to forget about their tax cuts, and to use the money to feed the hungry and to educate the poor. If they did not and sat on their high perches, history would repeat itself. They would be a Humpty Dumpty who took a great fall. Instead of leading his flock toward peace, George W. Bush chose a path to war.

The spate of terror spread with anthrax being sent through the mails from a post office in Hamilton Township, less than ten miles from my home in Princeton, New Jersey. The effects of hatred, vengeance, and a lack of world order hit close to home. Bioterrorism in the form of anthrax being sent through the mail caused a major panic reaction throughout the country. There was a fear that smallpox viruses would be the next to be unleashed.

Man's inhumanity to man was so evident. Greed, materialism, poverty, and squalor lived side by side, creating tension instead of relaxing it.

Marge Piercy wrote a poem, "The Fundamental Truth," which it was now appropriate to reflect upon.

> The Christian right, Islamic Jihad,
> The Jewish right bank settlers bringing
> The Messiah down, the Japanese sects
> Who worship by bombing subways
> They all hate each other.
> But more they hate the mundane,
> Ordinary people who love living
> More than dying in radiant glory,
> Who struggle and sigh and break bread.
>
> They need a planet of their own,
> Perhaps even a barren moon
> With artificial atmosphere,
> Where they will surely be nearer,
> To their gods and their fiercest
> Enemies where they can kill
> To their heart's peace
> Kill to the last standing man
> And leave the rest of us to be.

Not mystics to whom the holy,
Comes in the core of the struggle
In a shimmer of blinding quiet,
Not scholars haggling at the inner
Meaning of gnarly ancient sentences,
No, the holy comes to the zealots,
As a license to kill, for self-doubt,
And humility have dried like mud,
Under their marching feet.

They have far more in common,
With each other, there braggarts of
Hatred, the ironhearted,
In whose ear a voice spoke,

Once and left them deaf,
Their faith is founded on death
Of others, and everyone is other,
To them, whose Torah is splattered,
In letters of blood.

How prophetic was this poem written in the early 1990s!

A few months after September 11, people were bored with television news and its repetition of nonevents in Afghanistan. The country came out of shock and began to adapt to a new way of life.

A professor of Near East studies at Princeton, Richard Durand, explained to me the threat of fundamentalist Muslims. "They see democracy as anathema to the laws of Allah. The *umbal*, the idol, is like a law of man, contrary to the law of Allah. Transgressing Allah's law is punishable by death. Therefore, apostates, hypocrites, are punishable by destruction. Osama bin Laden called George W. Bush an *umbal*, a symbol of Western civilization. Therefore, Bush, a symbol of Western civilization is subject to destruction."

Bin Laden was fomenting revolution in Pakistan and Saudi Arabia, appealing to those poor who were oppressed by the regimes. Those who sided with the West were *umbals*. Bin Laden had created a cartoon of a man holding a shotgun trying to shoot a fly.

Terrorists, who thought of themselves as soldiers and martyrs, were in many places throughout the world. Bin Laden was no longer the charisma or brains behind Al Qaeda.

The television and newspapers broadcast and printed good news about the war on terrorism, but listeners and readers did not trust the media since it was becoming more and more viewed as a propaganda machine.

As winter set in, George W. Bush, John Ashcroft, and Donald Rumsfeld were a dangerous triumvirate. Yet the country joined in their very militant stance. They gave their performance a 92 percent approval rating. People responded to someone who was strong, and perhaps wrong, instead of to someone weak but right. The country was a flag-waving place, with lots of insecurity, calling for protection. In Afghanistan, bomb after bomb fell, while Special Forces tried to find Osama bin Laden.

The news became more and more violent. Bombs fell in the Tora Bora Mountains in Afghanistan. The Israelis and the Palestinians exchanged fireworks like it was the finale to a July Fourth display. Kashmiri terrorists conducted a suicide attack on the Indian Parliament. Bush pulled out of the Anti-Ballistic Missile Treaty of 1970 so that the United States could build a missile shield. The arms race was on again.

The surpluses garnered under Clinton turned to deficits faster than one could blink an eye.

The war in Afghanistan was almost over; and the questions that remained were, Where was Osama bin Laden, and where would George W. Bush go next?

The stock market, reflecting the fear, dove beneath 8,000. Dishonesty in business, especially the Tyco, Enron, and WorldCom scandals, consumed tons of ink and robbed investors and pensioners of their savings.

After the scandals, President Bush began to berate business in a way that Herbert Hoover did after the greed and dishonesty that pervaded the 1920s.

To deflect the public's attention to the economy, Bush began to saber rattle, urging the United Nations to disarm Saddam Hussein of Iraq. His speech at the United Nations was bellicose, but weak, as he argued that Hussein had disregarded the resolutions adopted by the United Nations in 1991 despite an embargo and arms inspections which revealed no violations. Instead of portraying the United States as a peace-loving, compassionate nation, he added to an image of the United States as a rogue nation. Bush, hypocritically, used the United Nations as a guise to make a first strike against Saddam Hussein.

In response, financial markets fell and interest rates plummeted to their lowest levels in thirty-nine years. The economy was on a precipice. Bush's policies gave India and China more opportunities to replace the United States as the powers in the twenty-first century. With their population, resources, talent, and cheap labor, India and China commoditized the technology industry and caused it to suffer the same fate as the United States' steel, auto, textile, and manufacturing industries did after Vietnam caused inflation and lack of focus.

Bush further placed the United States in the role of the world's policeman, instead of sharing that role with Europe, Russia, China, and Japan.

Rallies were held all over the world against an invasion of Iraq. Policies were beginning to encourage populists around the world to despise the United States and were imbuing a culture of fear in the country.

The unrest in the world continued to build. People over the world became more and more resigned to the reality and consequences of random attacks by the powerless who want the power.

The millennium had begun with a fear of Y2K, a worldwide chaos that would cause a worldwide breakdown. The event never happened. The economy appeared to be booming. The United States was flush with a surplus Who would have thought that two years later the world would be a bubbling cauldron of unrest?

Robert Kaplan's *Warrior Politics* reviewed political philosophers from Thucydides, Plato, and Machiavelli to Thomas Hobbes and Malthus and concluded that man will always war, that poverty and unemployment will, as it has in the past, lead to strife, and that the United States could no longer use the oceans as its shields and withdraw to safety after a battle. At the dawn of 2003, Kaplan's conclusions were reflected in a pall of frustration and hopelessness in the minds of the common man in the United States.

Had, as Kaplan wrote, the evils of the twentieth century arisen from populist movements that were then exploited in the name of utopian ideals, and had their power amplified by new technologies? Had not Nazism, Bolshevism, and Communism begun as crusades for workers' rights? Would peacemaking be any different because peacemaking required someone strong?

As I thought about our founders and Robert Kaplan's thesis, I realized that the United States had lost its focus on its national purpose. Instead of fighting to control the world, it had to battle to permit its people, as a government of the people, for the people, and by the people, to decide what they wanted to do, encouraging the American people to ask who they were, where do they fit in, and, more importantly, where they did not. Then and only then could the government decide what to do.

If the philosophers of the past were right, it was time to stop on a dime, rekindle memories, and work for change by focusing on Machiavelli's words, "Anyone wishing to see what is to be must consider what has been."

Interestingly, while the news reported the decimation of Al Qaeda, more and more leaders were saying that poverty was the cause of terrorism.

Instead of alienating the rest of the world with his bully tactics, saying, "I know what is right," Bush had to display humility, quoting from the Constitution, "We the people . . . in order to form a more perfect union," teaching the world what the United States has accomplished, where it has failed, stressing that it is forever trying to better the lot of people instead of creating turmoil in its quest for oil. Unfortunately, he did not.

I watched a Native American talk on C-SPAN about what her granny taught her. Water bugs were important because they purified the water. Forests and mountains were important because they purified the air. How sad it was that we were ruining the environment.

As it is true that only Muslims in Arab countries and Jews in Israel can root out terrorism by abhorring those within their midst that promote it, so it is that only Americans can root out the cause of their troubles – poverty.

That the future welfare of the United States and the world is going to be determined by the youth on the planet is a fact that no one can contest. What those in power are ignoring is the manner in which young people in the United States and throughout the world are being treated.

In July 2001, a one-hundred-page report entitled "Long-Term Global Demographic Trends: Reshaping the Geopolitical Landscape" was issued by the CIA. In a nutshell, what the report said is that dramatic population declines have created power vacuums that new ethnic groups exploit, that differential population growth rates between neighbors have historically altered conventional balances of power, and that our allies in the industrialized world will face an unprecedented challenge of aging.

The report goes on to say that "Europe and Japan stand to lose global power and influence and warns that the failure to integrate large youth populations in the Middle East and Sub-Saharan Africa is likely to perpetuate the cycle of political instability, ethnic wars, revolutions and anti-regime activities that already affects many of these countries. Unemployed youth provide exceptional fodder for radical movements and terrorist organizations, particularly in the Middle East."

Issued, as it was, before September 11, 2001, a date that will live in infamy, I thought about the report because the fodder of discontented youths mined by Osama bin Laden, by Hamas and other anti-Israel, anti-Western groups, and the fodder of discontented youths in Zimbabwe and its sub-Saharan neighbors has filled the pages of our newspapers and the screens of our television sets with scenes of violence.

A product of the '60s, I witnessed discontented youth ravage Trenton, my city. People in power who ignored the needs of those youth who rampaged downtown planted the seeds of that discontent.

Those in power are committing the same error, not only in our own country but also in countries throughout the Middle East and Africa.

The Bank Credit Analyst, a reputable population analyst, has projected that population of the industrial world countries will decline during the first half of this century. Those of the undeveloped countries will rise dramatically. Germany will remain at eighty million while Yemen will grow from eighteen to over eighty million. While Russia's population of one hundred fifty will lose fifty million, Iran will grow from sixty-five to over one hundred million. As Italy loses twelve of its fifty-seven million, Afghanistan's population will increase from twenty to seventy million. Iraq and Saudi Arabia will have one hundred ten million, the same number of people as Japan will have.

The countries that are increasing in population are predominantly Islamic. Is it any wonder that our political leaders are creating fear and hatred of Islamics for political gain? Politicians need enemies to solidify power.

Unfortunately, our political leaders have chosen the wrong enemy.

Instead of the unilateral, preemptive aggressive policy being pursued by Washington, and I include both parties, a policy that focuses on the employment of youth in this country, industrialized nations, and undeveloped nations must come to the fore – quickly.

I opposed preemptive aggression in Iraq. I supported increased inspections and the withdrawal of economic sanctions imposed on Iraq. Two important goals could have been achieved. First, inspections on a continuing basis would have neutralized any threat Saddam Hussein posed to the Free World. Secondly, trade with Iraq would have created jobs and intertwined our economy with that in Iraq.

Who, in 1945, would have predicted that regimented Japan would move toward democracy? Who would have thought that China and the United States would solve problems peacefully and that China would be moving toward democracy?

The interdependency of nations caused by free markets leads to a better chance for peace and democracy than missiles and bombs.

I have witnessed firsthand in India and Vietnam what can happen when government recognizes that an educated and employed youth can move its society toward internal security, prosperity, and peace.

Even though the leadership in Washington has alienated people throughout the world, it is not too late to reverse that trend.

Let us remove the tragedy of September 11 from our psyche and recognize that the seeds of the tragedy were planted by the industrial world's failure to create a Marshall Plan to lift up the youth in countries where dictators exploit for selfish reasons.

There is no room for regimes that do not recognize that winning a war against poverty is the only way for liberty and freedom to triumph. Nor is there time for us to be led much longer by leaders who do not take the risk to mend our ways with the youth that will determine the future for our children, grandchildren, and ourselves. That is the way to fight a war against terror through my lens.

LADDER TO LEGACY

My mind has been racing today. Newsclips show the devastation wrought by bombs in Afghanistan, Iraq, Pakistan, and India, targeting Muslims. I've been thinking about what to do with my thoughts – and the terror I am seeing through my lens. So I came up with an idea. Why not write a letter to my grandchildren, Noah, five years old, and Evan, three?

March 28, 2006

Dear Noah and Evan,

We are in the midst of a war against terror. But we need accurate information. While it is vital to know who your enemies are, it is just as important to know who they are not.

Only a tiny number of Muslims take part in acts of terror and violence. If our media and politicians continue to denigrate Islam, accepting without question the stereotype that Muslims are "anti-American," we will eventually alienate Muslims who have no quarrel with the West, who are either enjoying or longing for a greater democracy and who are horrified by the atrocities committed in the name of their faith.

One of the most important assets of the United States in its struggle against terrorism is the Muslim community in America. Many American Muslims treasure the fact that they can practice their religion far more creatively in the United States than in their countries of origin. We need to build bridges with them. We can not forget that at the time of our war for independence against Britain, a small percent of the colonists were Catholic and were hated and despised and thought to be opposed to freedom and democracy.

Just after 9-11-2001, Ellen and I were in Portugal and I wrote about how foolish it has been for the United States to support undemocratic regimes in the Middle East, failing to live up to our own ideals, unwittingly fostering the growth of extremism.

Atrocity leads to retaliation-attack to counterattack-to pre-emptive strike and a new state of terror. That is what has happened since 9-11.

Now we live in fear. Fear breeds a number of things – hatred of anything associated with the enemy – from their appearance to clothing to religion – and a circling of the wagon mentality.

I have tried to analyze how we have gotten to such a rise in Islamic religious fundamentalism. Perhaps it has been because of the rapid accumulation of Western wealth, fueled by democratic capitalism, and the perception that this wealth is used to aggravate the plight of the poor? Perhaps by the perception that Western nations restricted their political and military support to undemocratic regimes? Perhaps by the rise of a militant modern secularism which threatens traditional Islamic culture and religion?

Perhaps by the unnatural landscape the colonial powers left behind in splitting up the Middle East?

The Muslims I know want to be included as a full, welcome member of society, getting equal treatment from the United States and Europe. Right now, Muslims see that Turkey is being denied admission to the European Union because it is a predominantly Muslim country.

I believe that a good society needs to let all religions speak out. No religion – not even atheism – should be allowed to inhibit any other.

The word Islam in the Koran means "act of submission" to God. Practicing a religion is something you do. But today, religion is something you are. There is a danger in labeling things because labels begin to own you. A Muslim was used in the Koran to describe someone who "submitted to God." So devout Christians and Jews were Muslim. Today Islam and Muslim go together, not Islam and Jew or Islam or Christian.

Okay, we must acknowledge that there is conflict in the world today. Conflict has root causes. It is nearly always the loss of assets – A thing of value. An asset can be an idea, like losing your honor, the right to teach something or something that is a tangible idea – like an inheritance. Our beliefs are among our most treasured assets.

Another root cause of conflict is power – who gets to control decisions, who gets to decide what about what. Ellen and I argue about the color of a bathroom or a new carpet, where to go on vacation, or who puts out the garbage. Over time, a build up of such disagreements can lead to acrimony that puts us at odds. When we patch things up, we often ask, "Why were we fighting over this?"

In reality, we were fighting over who gets to decide what about what. The anger is not primarily about the carpet color! This is why we often end up saying, "Don't tell me what to do." We cherish the right to make our own decisions.

Once an argument is kindled, a psychological pattern develops in which we look at what differentiates us from the other side. This difference contributes to the otherness of our opponent and fuels the righteousness of our cause.

Violent conflict is nearly always related to a perceived injustice in the distribution of power and assets.

Many of us value ideas such as our own philosophy of life, our worldview. For most, atheists like me included, the most important values are those that, when violated or infringed, invoke the fight or flight syndrome.

The challenge to anyone involved in conflict resolution is always to find the underlying issues of power and assets. When a group or person is under attack, in order to survive, a certain amount of aggression in the name of God is bound to evolve. This defensive instinct is what leads to the rise of religious fundamentalism. Violence and chaos are unhealthy for society. People will fight for what they value personally. I am far more likely to become emotionally involved if someone throws a rock through my window than through a stranger's window. When our personal territory is transgressed, our buttons of aggressive and defensive conduct are pressed.

We humans have an unfortunate tendency to regard people of different religions, races and ethnic origins as almost different species.

In fighting for something, people will always justify their positions in terms of their deepest values, namely justice, truth, honor, freedom, national pride, or the protection of loved ones. For some, God is the All-being Creator, in whom is anchored their understanding of absolute justice, truth, love, etc.

Atheists, like me, who do not believe in the All Being Creator, nevertheless will fight for ideals of justice, truth, honor and democracy. It is perfectly logical that people will fight – often to the death for a God or a deep-seeded human value. I almost became a rabbi. But I became an atheist after learning about the Holocaust, when 6,000,000 Jews and millions of others, who were anathema to Hitler, were massacred. My disbelief in a God deepened as clients, one after another, innocents all, told me about the tragedy – the accident that in a mini-second changed their lives. "Unless," I said, "someone could prove to me there was a God, I could not believe there was one."

I believe you should fight in defense – if attacked – like being thrown out of a home or denied basic civil rights. Killing innocent people is never allowed. When people talk in the name of God, they are usually really doing so in the name of their ego, their struggle for power, or their desire to obtain some other asset.

In order to solve a dispute with Ellen, I have to see her point of view. Similarly, if we don't see why the Muslims who attack us are upset, we are likely to expand the chasm between us instead of building bridges.

My grandfather, Lou, used to quote an old Indian saying, "Don't criticize others until you have walked in their shoes." We need a new level of interfaith work between the media in both the Western and Muslim worlds that changes the discourse from "look how bad you are" to "look what we can do together."

I have learned that truth is not about facts. It is as much about how we perceive the facts. What I see as truth is often the interpretation of the facts, shaped by values so deeply imbedded in our subconscious that we don't see the other side's truth until an analogy in our own context opens our eyes.

I will close this letter saying that my history shapes how I continue to act. It is important for me to be aware of events in the past for they determine my attitudes and world views today. If I ignored my history, I would remain trapped in the past. I hope that you will do your best to discover history and learn through it to walk in the other guy's shoes. It is because of you and your generation that I still have hope that "we the people . . . can form a more perfect union," fighting terror with weapons used by your Great Grandfather Sidney – kindness, empowerment, guidance and humor.

Love,
Grandpa Albert

ACKNOWLEDGMENTS

While the observations that I recorded in my journal are my own, they were synthesized by the discussion of current events that I had with my wife, Ellen, at the breakfast table.

To Barbara Gitenstein, president of The College of New Jersey, and Professor of History, Alan Dawley, I thank you for creating a Center for Social Justice at TCNJ. In appreciation, the proceeds earned by this book will be donated to the Center for Social Justice.

To Nancy Karlosky, my assistant for the past forty years, I thank you for your patience and proofreading. Without the help of Debbie Graiff's tutelage in Word, I would not have been able to fight the terror I experienced when pages and paragraphs appeared on the screen in the most unexpected places.

My thanks to Molly Davis, who read my manuscript and added the chapter titles.

To Irwin Rosenblum and Mort Zachter, I say thanks for reading and giving me honest feedback.

To Sherwin Soy, Christine Gerra, Kevin Desabelle, and Azela Jane P. Erasga, my helpers at Xlibris, I am forever indebted for your professional help in copyediting, cover design and layout.

Albert M. Stark
March 2006